What?

A DRAGON Question Book™

By Kathie Billingslea Smith
Illustrated by Robert S. Storms

A DRAGON BOOK

GRANADA

What is sign language?

Many people in the world do not hear very well. Some of them cannot talk at all or hear what other people say.

So these people talk another way — with their hands! They use sign language. They make pictures or signs with their hands to show different words and ideas.

The sign for "wake up" looks like you are opening your eyes with your fingers.

This sign means "love." It looks like a hug!

Lots of other people "talk" without speaking: American Indians used to talk with their hands when they did not know the language of another Indian tribe.

Today, umpires use special signs during cricket games.

Traffic officers "talk" to drivers by blowing on whistles and holding up gloved hands to say, "STOP!"

We all use our hands and bodies to talk with other people.

We point our fingers, rub our stomachs, shrug our shoulders, and shake our heads. Can you think of other signs that you make?

What makes puddle

After a rainstorm, you can see many puddles on the ground. As time goes by, the puddles get smaller and smaller until they finally disappear. What makes this happen?

As the sun shines on the ground, it heats up the water in the puddles. The water becomes so warm that it changes into a gas called water vapour. This changing action is called evaporation.

disappear?

You cannot see the water vapour because it becomes part of the air. The water from the puddles evaporates into the air a little at a time until the puddle is gone.

Water evaporates from puddles, and from ponds, rivers,

and oceans too. When it reaches the cool air high above the earth, the water vapour changes back into tiny drops of water. All the drops stick together to form a cloud. The drops grow heavier and heavier until at last it rains. Then you have puddles to splash in once again!

When you read stories or write words, do you ever wonder which letters are used most often?

The letter **e** is found more often than any other letter in the alphabet.

Elephants **e**xercise **e**arly in th**e e**v**e**ning — if th**e**y hav**e** any **e**n**e**rgy at all.

These letters, in the order of how often they are used, are also found many times:

nost often in words?

t a i s o and **n**. Can you think of words that start with each of these letters? **Think about it. . .**

Now, can you guess which letter is used the least? It's the letter **z**! In fact, the letter **e** is used fifty times more often then the letter **z**. Knowing this might help you when you play a game of hangman!

What is the fastes

The fastest land animal is the cheetah. Over a short distance, it can run as fast as 112 km per hour! Deer and antelopes are also swift runners with top speeds of between 80 and 96 km per hour. People, when they are running their very fastest, can only go about 35 km per hour.

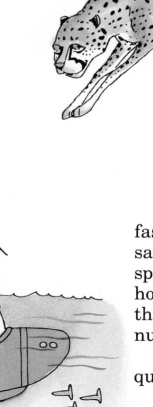

In the ocean, the fastest fish is the sailfish. It can swim at speeds of 109 km per hour. This is much faster than any of the world's nuclear submarines can go!

Dragonflies can move more quickly than any other insect.

They can fly at speeds of 56 km per hour.

But the world's fastest creatures are two birds: the swift and the peregrine falcon. Both birds can easily fly more than 160 km per hour. Scientists design jet planes to have the same shape as these birds with their pointed, swept-back wings. When the peregrine falcon takes a power dive, it folds its wings against its body. It can then move at speeds of more than 320 km per hour, zooming towards the ground!

What cause

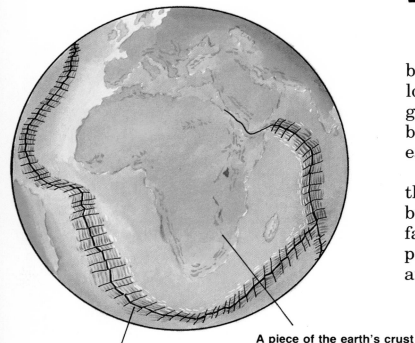

A piece of the earth's crust

Where two pieces meet

bumping and grinding cause a lot of pressure under the ground. When the pressure becomes too great, we have an earthquake.

During a strong earthquake, the ground shakes and the earth buckles. Sometimes buildings fall down, hurting or killing people. Sometimes whole cities are destroyed.

The crust which covers our earth is like a huge puzzle made of many pieces. These pieces move very slowly. Where two pieces meet, they grind and rub against each other. The

earthquakes?

Scientists are learning more and more about earthquakes. They use a special machine called a seismograph to help them. They know why earthquakes happen and where they are likely to take place. But scientists cannot always tell *when* earthquakes will hit.

When something bothers the inside of your nose, you sneeze to get rid of it.

Inside your nose are lots of tiny hairs. These hairs help clean the air that you breathe into your body. The hairs catch dust and other small things that are in the air.

nose

A-a-a--CH o o o!

Sometimes the dust will tickle the inside of your nose. When that happens, look out — then you'll — have — to — snee — A-a-a-choo!

You also sneeze when you have a cold or hay fever. Then the inside of your nose swells up and hurts.

A-a-a--CH O O O!

Sneezes help to clean out your nose and make you feel better. But germs and dust are blown out of your nose and mouth when you sneeze. That is why it is good to cover up sneezes with a tissue or with your hand!

Look at a pencil. The outside part that you hold is made of wood.

Inside the wood is a thin gray stick of graphite. Graphite is made up of tiny crystals of carbon, a black material. These crystals are shaped so that they can easily be rubbed away from one another. When you write with a pencil, the marks that the pencil makes are just tiny pieces of graphite that stick where the pencil pushes against the paper.

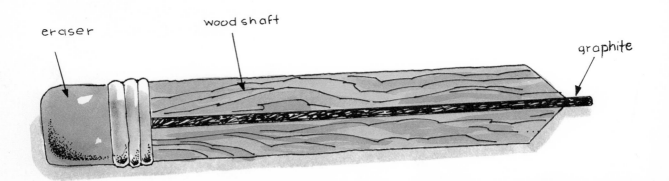

eraser

wood shaft

graphite

pencil write?

After you write with a pencil for a while, the graphite on the tip of the pencil gets worn away. Then you need to sharpen your pencil to help the graphite touch the paper again.

Winter can be a problem time for animals. The weather is cold and often snowy. Food and water are hard to find.

Some birds fly south to warmer lands where there is plenty of food. This is called migration. Some fish also migrate southward — to warmer waters.

Deer and wolves and foxes grow thick coats of fur to keep themselves warm.

In the north, the fur of rabbits and weasels changes from brown to white. This helps them hide from their enemies.

Raccoons, skunks, and bears take long naps in their dens.

do in winter?

spring. They live this way all winter on the fat stored in their bodies and wake up in the spring when it is warm again.

Now and then, they wake up to hunt for food.

Chipmunks and groundhogs are some of the biggest sleepers! In the autumn, they stuff themselves with food until they can hardly walk, then find a warm spot under the ground and *hibernate*, or sleep, until

What does the bottom o

Much of the earth is covered by oceans.

Near the shore, an ocean is not very deep. The ocean bottom there is like a big shelf of land covered with rocks, sand, and seaweed. Many different kinds of fish and plants live there.

The middle part of an ocean is very, very deep. Red clay covers most of the sea bottom there. This part of an ocean is cold and dark. The light of the sun

he ocean look like?

cannot reach there because the ocean is so deep. Plants on the bottom of the ocean are white like mushrooms. Fish cannot see on the ocean bottom because there is no light, but they smell and touch all around them to find food. Many of these fish are strange-looking with huge jaws or oddly shaped bodies. Some of them give off bright lights, which they use to draw other fish over who will become dinner.

You have 206 bones in your body — bones of different shapes and sizes. These bones are all joined together to form your skeleton.

Bones are hard and stiff. They help protect your heart and lungs and brain and other parts of your body.

Your backbone lets you bend . . .

Muscles are attached to your bones. Whenever you want to walk, or even scratch your head, your muscles pull on your bones to move just the right part of your body — a finger, a toe, an arm, a foot.

The 33 bones in your backbone, or spine, are the most important bones in your body.

mportant bones
in your body?

You have bones . . .

These bones are separate, yet they are joined together by muscles to form a long, bony tube from the base of your skull down to your lower back. These bones, or *vertebrae*, as they are called, help you to stand up straight, but they also allow you to move easily and to bend.

Why, without your backbone, you would fall over in a heap!

But a jellyfish doesn't . . .

What happens while

While you are asleep, many people are busy!

Post office workers are sorting mail for the next day's delivery.

Grocery workers are putting food on the shelves.

Doctors and nurses are awake too. They are helping people who are sick.

'm asleep?

Police officers and firemen are watching over the town while you sleep.

In factories, many people are building cars and tools and other products.

All through the night, trucks and trains and planes are carrying post and supplies and people to different places.

And while it is night here, it is daytime on the other side of the world. People there are going to school and working just as we do here during the day. When you wake up in the morning, they are getting ready for bed!

What are freckles?

Everyone has skin with tiny grains of colouring in it. This colouring is called melanin. People with dark skins have a lot of melanin. People with light skins do not have much melanin.

In some people, the melanin is gathered in spots. These spots are called freckles.

Some people are born with freckles. Others get freckles after they have been outside on a bright sunny day.

Look closely at your skin. Do you have freckles?